GEO
NA
USA PARKS
OLYMPIC
Olympic

Olympic National Park

John Hamilton

VISIT US AT

WWW.ABDOPUB.COM

Published by ABDO Publishing Company, 8000 West 78th Street, Suite 310, Edina, MN 55439.
Copyright ©2009 by Abdo Consulting Group, Inc. International copyrights reserved in all countries.
No part of this book may be reproduced in any form without written permission from the publisher.
ABDO & Daughters™ is a trademark and logo of ABDO Publishing Company.

Printed in the United States.

Editor: Sue Hamilton
Graphic Design: John Hamilton
All photos and illustrations by the author, except p. 5 mountain lake, National Park Service; p. 9 map,
National Park Service; p. 12 fish illustration, National Park Service; p. 13 (top) Joseph P. O'Neil,
courtesy Robert B. Hitchman; p. 13 (bottom) fisherwoman, National Park Service; p. 14 blood star,
National Park Service; p. 20 skier, National Park Service; p. 22 elk, National Park Service; p. 28 spotted
owl, National Park Service; p. 29 Robert geranium, courtesy Oregon State University.

Library of Congress Cataloging-in-Publication Data

Hamilton, John, 1959-
  Olympic National Park / John Hamilton.
      p. cm. -- (National parks)
  Includes index.
  ISBN 978-1-60453-093-3
  1. Olympic National Park (Wash.)--Juvenile literature. I. Title.

  F897.O5H36 2009
  979.7'98--dc22
                                        2008011891

Contents

Left: Tourists at the Hurricane Ridge Visitor Center watch the Olympic Mountains at sunset.

Forest meets ocean at Olympic National Park's **Ruby Beach.**

Three Parks in One

When paying the entrance fee to Olympic National Park, visitors get three parks for the price of one. Set in Washington's rugged Olympic Peninsula, the park is home to three distinct ecosystems: craggy mountains, temperate rain forests, and rugged seashore. Ambitious tourists can sample all three in a single day, but wise visitors take their time, absorbing the many sights and sounds this magnificent place has to offer. It's like a living laboratory for everybody to explore.

On the seashore, salt-laden air blows in from the Pacific Ocean. Waves crash against 57 miles (92 km) of untamed shoreline. At low tide, miniature universes of life exist in pools of water left stranded by the receding ocean. Starfish, sea anemones, barnacles, and other creatures find shelter here. High above, sea gulls compete with bald eagles for control of the skies. In the water, harbor seals and otters frolic. Farther out to sea, California gray whales are often spotted during their spring and winter migrations.

In the wild interior rise massive snow-capped peaks called the Olympic Mountains, for which the park is named. The highest of these is Mount Olympus, soaring 7,980 feet (2,432 m) high. Several glaciers are draped on the mountain's shoulders, fed by moist ocean winds that drop almost 200 inches (508 cm) of precipitation each year, most of it snow. Distinctive U-shaped valleys radiate from the mountains, harboring lakes, wetlands, and meadows. Olympic marmots, unique to this area, make their home in the high country.

Only 33 miles (53 km) of land separates Mount Olympus from the Pacific Ocean. Between these two extremes is a landscape so rich and diverse that there are few like it anywhere in the world. This temperate rain forest averages more than 12 *feet* (3.7 m) of rain each year. The geography of this Pacific Northwest landscape creates an almost perpetual mist and rain. Moss and vines hang from the trees. Decaying organic matter on the forest floor is thicker than that found in most tropical rain forests. Giants live here. There are 10 trees found in the park that hold world records for being the largest of their kind. Many cedars and fir trees rise up 250 feet (76 m) or more. Sheltered in this old-growth forest community are many kinds of animals, from black bear and Roosevelt elk, to hummingbirds and owls. Rushing rivers, fed by mountain glaciers, flow through the forest, many filled with trout and salmon.

The great majority of Olympic is sheltered wilderness, with many plants and animals found nowhere else in the world. So much of the park is unspoiled that it has been named an international biosphere reserve and a World Heritage Site by the United Nations. These designations give the parkland even more protection.

U.S. Highway 101 runs around three sides of the park. Spur roads, like spokes of a giant wheel, venture into the interior for a few miles, then abruptly stop at trailheads. Exploring more of the park requires wilderness camping, or at least a day hike. More than 600 miles (966 km) of paths crisscross the park. Most of the 3.3 million annual visitors will soak up the view from their cars. But for adventurous souls, hiking into the rough, tough backcountry of Olympic National Park is no chore; it is the trip of a lifetime.

Left: Dense vegetation covers the ground of the Hoh Rain Forest.

Wildflowers bloom in a meadow along **Hurricane Ridge.**

Geology and Weather

Like a giant thumb sticking out of Washington's northwest corner, the Olympic Peninsula is a wild, isolated place. Olympic National Park, which occupies more than 922,00 acres (373,000 ha) of federal land, is one of the biggest in the national park system. About 95 percent of Olympic is designated wilderness, yet the nearest major city, Seattle, Washington, is only 40 miles (64 km) away.

The park is truly epic in scale, literally *Olympian*. Named after the sanctuary of Zeus and other ancient Greek gods, Olympic is a wilderness shelter, untamed and unspoiled thanks to its remote location and the foresight of those who preserved it for future generations.

The Olympic Mountains get so much rain because of their geography. Moisture-rich clouds blowing in from the Pacific Ocean are forced upward by the steep mountains. Once cooled, the clouds can no longer hold much of their rain. More than 135 inches (243 cm) of moisture falls each year on the western slopes. No other spot in the contiguous United States gets as much. But because of the rain shadow effect, slopes on the eastern side of the mountains don't receive nearly as much rain.

The mountains in the center of Olympic weren't always so lofty. Clues can be found in the basalt and sedimentary rock, in which sharp-eyed geologists find fossils of prehistoric sea creatures. Approximately 30 million years ago, the area was a vast plain on the ocean floor. Then, two enormous tectonic plates collided. The edge of one plate was thrust upward over a period of millions of years, creating the mountains. Glaciers carved and polished the rocks, and also created Puget Sound and the Strait of Juan de Fuca. Partially isolated from the mainland, life on the Olympic Peninsula evolved into unique species found nowhere else on Earth, such as the Olympic marmot, Crescenti trout, and the Olympic torrent salamander.

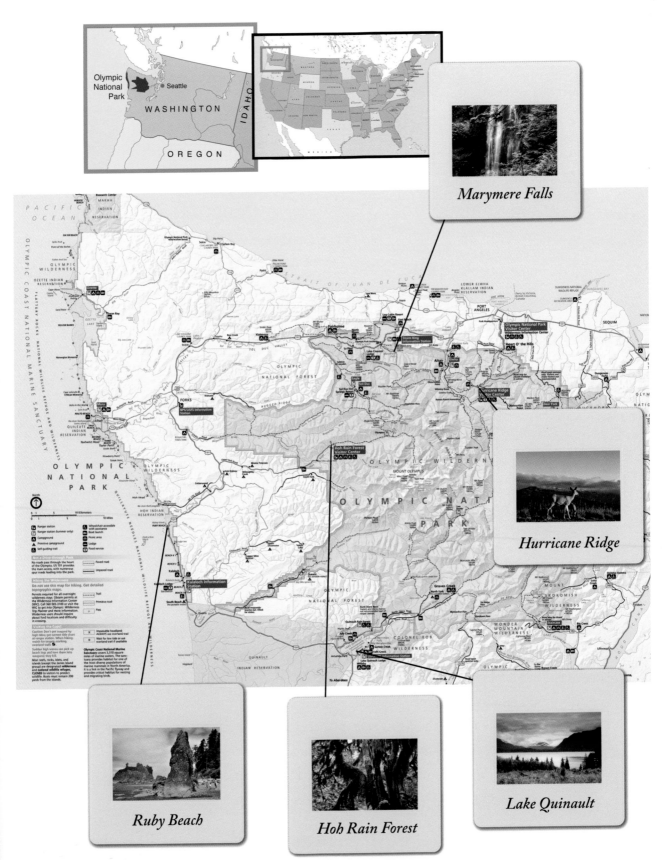

Marymere Falls

Hurricane Ridge

Ruby Beach

Hoh Rain Forest

Lake Quinault

9

"Climb the mountains and get their good tidings..."

—John Muir *(Above: The Olympic Mountains as seen from Hurricane Ridge at dusk.)*

History in the Park

The earliest residents of the Olympic Peninsula were Native Americans who arrived in the area about 12,000 years ago. At that time, vast ice-age glaciers were in retreat. Roaming the landscape were mastodons, elk, bison, and wolves. We know that Native Americans hunted in Olympic because of what a farmer found in 1977. Digging in a pond just outside the park, the man found the remains of a prehistoric, elephant-like mammal—a mastodon. Imbedded in the animal's ribs was a broken spear point, evidence of early human hunters who relied on the game-rich landscape.

About 3,000 years ago, the population of Native American groups increased. Instead of following migrating herds of animals, these people lived in villages belonging to eight distinct tribes: the Hoh, Jamestown S'Klallam, Elwha Klallam, Makah, Port Gamble S'Klallam, Quileute, Quinault, and Skokomish.

Instead of relying only on hunting, these tribes also harvested the rivers and oceans. The Makah are famous for their tradition of whaling. The tribes also used items found in the forests to make shelter and medicine. Cedar trees were an important resource, used to make canoes, house planks, and many other items. Crafts such as woven baskets and tools made of shells are found at archaeological sites inside the park.

The first European to see the Olympic Peninsula was probably Juan de Fuca. He was a Greek ship pilot who sailed for Spain. He came to the area in 1592. The Strait of Juan de Fuca, to the north of the park, now bears his name. Spanish explorer Juan Perez Hernandez sailed along the Olympic coast in 1774. In 1788, awestruck English explorer Captain John Meares gave the mountains their name. He called the tallest peak Mount Olympus, comparing it to the legendary Greek home of the gods.

The Olympic Peninsula has always been a wild and rugged place, difficult to explore. In 1885, American Lieutenant Joseph P. O'Neil led the first well-documented exploration of the northern Olympic Mountains. His group struggled a full month to ascend Hurricane Ridge from Port Angeles, a trip that motorists can complete today in less than one hour. In 1890, O'Neil went on a second expedition, this time exploring the eastern and southern part of the peninsula. In his report, O'Neil wrote, "In closing I would

Joseph O'Neil

state that while the country on the outer slope of these mountains is valuable, the interior is useless for all practicable purposes. It would, however, serve admirably for a national park."

By the mid-19th century, towns had sprung up along the coast of the Olympic Peninsula, including Port Angeles, Neah Bay, Sequim, and Port Townsend. Despite early promise, mass settlement never occurred; the area was just too rainy and thick with vegetation for farming. But logging and hunting, especially elk, soon became big business.

In 1909, President Theodore Roosevelt declared that a portion of the peninsula should be set aside to protect the forests and elk herds. Mount Olympus National Monument gave the area some protection, but logging restrictions were controversial.

Above: A fisherwoman with a freshly caught salmon.

After nearly three decades of struggle between logging businesses and conservation groups, Olympic National Park was created in 1938, signed into law by President Franklin Roosevelt. A strip of rugged coastline was added to the park in 1953.

In 1976, the United Nations added Olympic to its international list of Biosphere Preserves. These places are special because of their scientific and scenic value. In 1981, the United Nations declared the park to be a World Heritage Site. Like the pyramids of Egypt, these places are older than mere nations, and belong, symbolically at least, to the entire world.

The Seashore

Blood star

Even though there are hundreds of miles of trails that penetrate the interior wilderness of Olympic National Park, the single memory that many visitors cherish is strolling along the beach. The park protects 73 miles (117 km) of Pacific coast. Highway 101 makes about 10 miles (16 km) of southern beach accessible by car. To see the rest, you have to proceed on foot. It's a rare experience to witness so much unspoiled coastline.

The seashore is a narrow strip of land unconnected to the main body of the park. With the Pacific Ocean on one side and Olympic National Forest on the other, the wild coastline shelters an abundance of marine life. Southern beaches are sandy, while beaches in the north of the park are rockier. Just offshore are sentinel-like sea stacks. These tall, rocky outcroppings are miniature islands cut off from the mainland by the constant battering of the ocean. Seabirds, seals, and sea lions make their homes here. Often shrouded in rain or mist, the coast has a fantasyland feel to it. When the summer sun decides to shine, it's a beach-lover's paradise.

Cold, nutrient-rich waters rising from the bottom of the Pacific Ocean feed an abundance of life along the coast. When the ocean pulls back at low tide, standing pools of water are left behind. Called tide pools, these miniature ecosystems are filled with colorful life. A pool of just one square foot (.09 sq m) might contain 4,000 tiny creatures jostling for space. Peer into any tide pool and you'll likely spot starfish, sea stars, mollusks, barnacles, sea urchins, and green sea anemones.

Anemone

Children splash along the **Seashore.**

Bald eagles nest on the tall trees bordering the beach. Sandpipers skitter across the sandy beaches. Heard over the roar of the surf is the screeching of ever-present seagulls. These birds have developed an ingenious method of foraging for a meal: from a height of 50 feet (15 m) or more, they drop clams onto the rocks below, busting them open. The gulls then dive down for a tasty treat.

Seagull

Camping is a popular activity along the coast, although many people simply stay for the day. There are miles of paths that follow the beach and wind through the adjacent forest. Before venturing into the wilderness coast, it's important to obtain a current tide table to make your hike as safe as possible.

At high tide, people can get trapped between the ocean and high cliffs. Floating drift logs, some as big as smokestacks, can also be hazardous when unexpected waves send them crashing to shore. Smart visitors stay aware of their surroundings so they can safely enjoy this rare wilderness.

Left: Beachcombers wander along a section of Olympic's Ruby Beach. Drift logs lie stranded on the beach at low tide.

On the south side of the park, the coastal beaches are mostly sand and pebbles (above). Hikers inspect a sea stack (below), a rocky outcropping caused by erosion from the ocean.

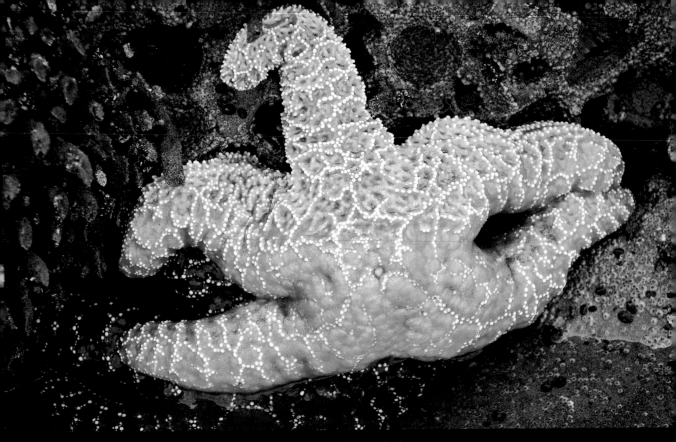

A starfish clings to a rock on the edge of a tide pool (above), home to many sea creatures. Marymere Falls (below) is easily reached by a trail starting on the edge of Lake Crescent.

Pine needles mix with maple leaves, backlit by the sun, in this scene from the Hoh Rain Forest (above). Sunset at Hurricane Ridge, overlooking the Olympic Mountains (below).

Mountains and Lakes

Olympic National Park's visitor center is located just south of the coastal town of Port Angeles. The easiest gateway to the park's mountainous interior is to take the 17-mile (27 km) road south to Hurricane Ridge. The road winds through forested lowlands all the way up to a subalpine region nearly one mile (1.6 km) high. On a clear day, the views are spectacular. The blue waters of the Strait of Juan de Fuca are visible to the north. To the south rise the mountains of the snow-capped Bailey Range, with Mount Olympus soaring 7,980 feet (2,432 m) just behind them.

Hurricane Ridge gets its name from the winds that blow through in winter, bringing with them piles of snow. Mount Olympus receives about 200 inches (508 cm) of precipitation each year. There are 60 major glaciers in the park. Seven of them are wrapped around the shoulders of Mount Olympus, including Blue Glacier.

Skiing and snowshoeing are popular activities along Hurricane Ridge in the winter. During summer, many people leave their cars and hike into the backcountry. Although the highest peaks are too rugged for most people to conquer, beautiful meadows and lakes abound in the lower elevations. The park has an extensive trail system. For those wishing simply to sightsee, the Hurricane Ridge Visitor Center has a series of nearby walking paths. Many people are happy to relax at the visitor center and gaze at the mountains, which seem to change character from minute to minute, depending on the weather.

Left: A cross-country skier takes a break to enjoy the Olympic Mountain scenery.

A deer and her fawn (above) graze along Hurricane Ridge, overlooking the Olympic Mountains. Lake Quinault (below), with the Olympic Mountains in the background.

Above: A herd of Roosevelt elk.

An alpine ecosystem exists near the top of Olympic's snow-capped peaks. Conditions here are cold and windy, making it difficult for life to find a foothold. Lichens and tiny ferns cling to the thin mountain soil. Chipmunks and marmots skit among the rocks. Golden eagles and ravens soar high above.

Farther down in elevation is the subalpine zone, a transition between the harsh alpine and the forests below the treeline. Although it is still cold here, with a short growing season, the soil is rich enough to support some trees and animals. Wildflowers abound, splashing bright color against the hills. Black-tailed deer, snowshoe hare, and black bear make their homes here. The Olympic marmot makes a distinctive whistle when disturbed. The park also protects the largest herd of Roosevelt elk in the world. The visitor center at Hurricane Ridge is a good starting point to explore subalpine wilderness.

After experiencing Olympic's high country, many people go back down the mountain to sample the dense forests of the lower elevations, especially the many paths and sights along the northern edge of the park. The old growth, lowland forests thrive in this mild climate, which provides deep soil and generous rainfall. Douglas firs and western hemlocks older than 200 years soar 30 stories tall, wider than three cars side-by-side. Trails along Lake Crescent or Sol Duc allow visitors to walk among these giants.

Lake Crescent was carved by a glacier long ago. Its deep, blue waters today are filled with trout. Highway 101 skirts the southern edge of the lake. At the halfway point, a pleasant 1.75-mile (2.82 km) path takes visitors through the forest alongside Barnes Creek to Marymere Falls, a sparkling 90-foot (27-m) waterfall that cuts a path through a blanket of green foliage (see photo on page 18).

There are many other waterfalls in the park, the most famous being Sol Duc Falls, just south of Sol Duc Hot Springs Resort. After a long day of hiking, many people enjoy pampering their tired muscles by soaking in the natural hot springs.

A hiker crosses a log bridge over **Barnes Creek**

The Rain Forest

When people think of rain forests, they usually imagine tropical jungles dripping with moisture, with monkeys chattering in the treetops. But several rain forests also exist in northern latitudes. These are called temperate rain forests. Olympic National Park preserves one of the biggest and most diverse in the world. Pacific Ocean storms dump much of their rain on the west-facing valleys of the Olympic Mountains. The forests receive 140 to 167 inches (356 to 424 cm) of rain each year.

Plants and trees grow at massive rates in Olympic's rain forests. The soil is thick and rich with biomass, dead plants that living organisms use to thrive. The cool temperatures and abundant rainfall make for perfect growing conditions. Mosses, ferns, and lichens grow freely on tree trunks, sometimes hanging, jungle-like, all the way to the ground. Plants that grow on other plants are called epiphytes, and give the rain forests their characteristic look.

Sitka spruce and western hemlock dominate the forest, but there are many other species here as well, including fir, maple, and cedar. Trees can live for hundreds of years in the rain forest, reaching up to 60 feet (18 m) around. When these giants finally topple over, it takes centuries for them to fully decay into the soil. Seedlings

often grow on these "nurse logs." Small mammals, amphibians, and insects also rely on the dead logs for habitat. Roosevelt elk graze on the forest floor, helping keep it open for new growth.

Left: Nurse logs help new trees to grow, as well as shelter animals and insects.

A moss-covered tree in the **Hoh Rain Forest.**

There are four major valleys in Olympic that harbor temperate rain forests: Quinault, Queets, Hoh, and Bogachiel. Most tourists make the long drive along Hoh Road to the Hoh Rain Forest Visitor Center. The center includes many exhibits and helpful forest rangers to answer questions. There are two main trails to sample the rain forest. The Hall of Mosses is an easy .8-mile (1.3-km) loop. The Spruce Nature Trail is slightly longer at 1.2 miles (1.9 km). Both trails meander through a wonderland of moss-covered trees and dense underbrush. Vines, ferns, and mosses give the forest an emerald color. It is often rainy or misty here. When the sun peeks out, shafts of gold cut through the canopy. High in the tree branches, spotted owls, bluebirds, finches, and hummingbirds produce flashes of color. Foraging on the forest floor are many animals, the largest including black bear and Roosevelt elk.

Hikers wishing for more adventure can continue on the Hoh River Trail. This 17-mile (27-km) path winds its way up to Glacier Meadows, which mountaineers often use as a staging area for a climb atop nearby Mount Olympus. Wilderness camping and fishing are allowed, but free permits should be obtained at the visitor center in advance. Trout and salmon fishing is excellent in the Hoh River.

Left: A moss-covered phone booth at the Hoh Rain Forest Visitor Center.

A woodpecker searches for food on a tree trunk in the **Hoh Rain Forest.**

Future Challenges

Before people began massive logging efforts, temperate rain forests were common along coastal ranges. Today, only a few protected areas remain. Along with Olympic, these include spots in New Zealand, southern Australia, and Chile. Despite the park's protected status, there is always human pressure that threatens to alter the landscape.

Early in Olympic's history, the timber industry resisted setting aside the land as a national park. The area's huge logs were very profitable to harvest, despite the remote location. Even though the parkland is protected today, logging continues in adjacent National Forest Service land. In recent years, logging on federal lands has been further restricted because of its impact on some plants and animals. The endangered northern

Spotted Owl

spotted owl, for example, depends on old-growth forests for its habitat. Logging restrictions were a hardship to neighboring communities, but many have adapted by offering services to visiting tourists.

Left: A section of forest that has been clear cut in Olympic National Forest, adjacent to Olympic National Park.

Olympic National Park attracts about 3.3 million visitors each year. Like many national parks, Olympic struggles with budget cuts at the same time it tries to accommodate visitors. Some areas, such as popular beaches in the south coastal area, can be very crowded in the busy summer season.

Tourists aren't the only invaders on the Olympic Peninsula. Park officials are increasingly worried about non-native plants and animals that have been released into the wilderness. Aggressive weedy plants, such as the Robert geranium, choke out native species in the forest underbrush. Mountain goats, released by early residents, today wreak havoc in the park's alpine region, destroying the delicate plants that live

Robert geranium

there. These and other non-native species are closely monitored by park officials, but controlling their numbers is a difficult task. These and other challenges stretch the resources of the National Park Service, but it's a battle worth fighting, in one of the nation's most treasured places.

Left: About 3.3 million people visit Olympic National Park each year.

Glossary

Alpine

In high mountains, alpine is the vegetation zone above the treeline, where it is too cold for trees to grow.

Ecosystem

A biological community of animals, plants, and bacteria, all of whom live together in the same physical or chemical environment.

Federal Lands

Much of America's land, especially in the western part of the country, is maintained by the United States federal government. These are public lands owned by all U.S. citizens. There are many kinds of federal lands. National parks, like Olympic National Park, are federal lands that are set aside so that they can be preserved. Other federal lands, such as national forests or national grasslands, are used in many different ways, including logging, ranching, and mining. Much of the land surrounding Olympic National Park is maintained by the government, including several national forests and wildlife refuges.

Forest Service

The United States Department of Agriculture (USDA) Forest Service was started in 1905 to manage public lands in national forests and grasslands. The Forest Service today oversees an area of 191 million acres (77.3 million hectares), which is an amount of land about the same size as Texas. In addition to protecting and managing America's public lands, the Forest Service also conducts forestry research and helps many state government and private forestry programs.

Glacier

A glacier is often called a river of ice. It is made of thick sheets of ice and snow. Glaciers slowly move downhill, scouring and smoothing the landscape.

RAIN SHADOW EFFECT

An effect that happens when clouds are forced to climb higher as they blow past mountains. As the clouds climb, water they contain condenses and falls as rain. After the clouds make it over the mountains, much of their moisture has been lost. Land on the other side of the mountains therefore receives much less rain.

SUBALPINE

A growth zone in the mountains that exists just below the treeline.

WETLAND

A wetland, sometimes called riparian, is an area of land that usually has standing water for most of the year, like swamps or marshes. Many wetlands have been set aside as preserves for wildlife. Many kinds of birds and animals depend on this habitat for nesting, food, and shelter.

Above: A deer grazes peacefully at the Storm King Ranger Station, near the southeast shore of Lake Crescent. An easy trail leads from here to Marymere Falls.

Index